15

RECORD BREAKERS

HUMAN BODY

DAVID JEFFERIS

Belitha Press

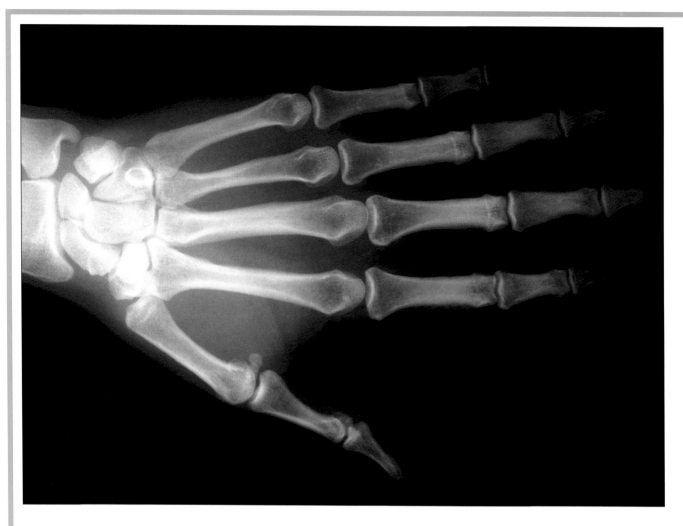

First published in the UK in 2002 by

Ⓑ Belitha Press

A member of **Chrysalis** Books plc

64 Brewery Road, London N7 9NT

Design and editorial production
Alpha Communications
Copyright © David Jefferis 2002

ISBN 1 84138 424 0

British Library Cataloguing in Publication
Data for this book is available from the
British Library.

10 9 8 7 6 5 4 3 2 1

Acknowledgements
We wish to thank the following
individuals and organizations for their
help and assistance and for supplying
material in their collections:
Alpha Archive, John Bavosi,
Nathan Benn, Lester B. Bergman,
Bettmann/Corbis, BSIP/Jacopin,
BSIP/Vero/Carlo, Jan Butchofsky-Houser,
CNRI, Corbis Images, David Gifford,
Mehau Kulyk, Peter Lomas/Rex
Features, Prof. P. Motta/Dept. of
Anatomy/University 'La Sapienza' Rome,
National Cancer Institute, NIBSC,
Dr. Yorgos Nikas, PIR-CNRI,
Alfred Pasteka, Catherine
Pouedras/Eurelios, Quest,
Science Photo Library, Volker Steger

Diagrams by Gavin Page
Project modelling by
Emily Stapleton-Jefferis
Educational advisor Julie Stapleton

We have checked the records in this
book but new ones are often added.

Printed in Taiwan

▲ The bones of a hand shown
in an x-ray picture. This type of
see-through photography was first
developed over 100 years ago by
Wilhelm Roentgen of Germany.

CONTENTS

👪 LOOK FOR THE FAMILY SYMBOL

Look for the family group in boxes like this.
Here you will find extra facts and records.

CELLS AND BONES

hard bone

spongy bone

bone marrow

▲ Bigger bones have marrow in the middle where blood cells are produced and fat stored.

We are made of billions of tiny cells. They are building blocks that form everything from bones and blood to ears and eyes.

Almost all cells are too small to see without a microscope – most are only about 0.03 mm in diameter. Cells carry out many jobs – for example, nerve cells carry messages around the body at up to 120m a second.

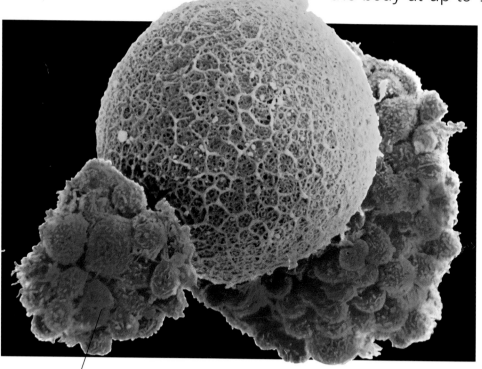

◄ The biggest cell of all is the egg, shown yellow in this view. Here it has been enlarged about 800 times but the real thing is smaller than this dot. When a smaller male sperm cell meets an egg they may join to create new life, the only cells to do so.

these cells support the egg

Our skeletons support and protect soft body organs, such as the brain, as well as anchoring our muscles. Inside many bones, marrow is hard at work making red blood cells – about 10 million of them every second.

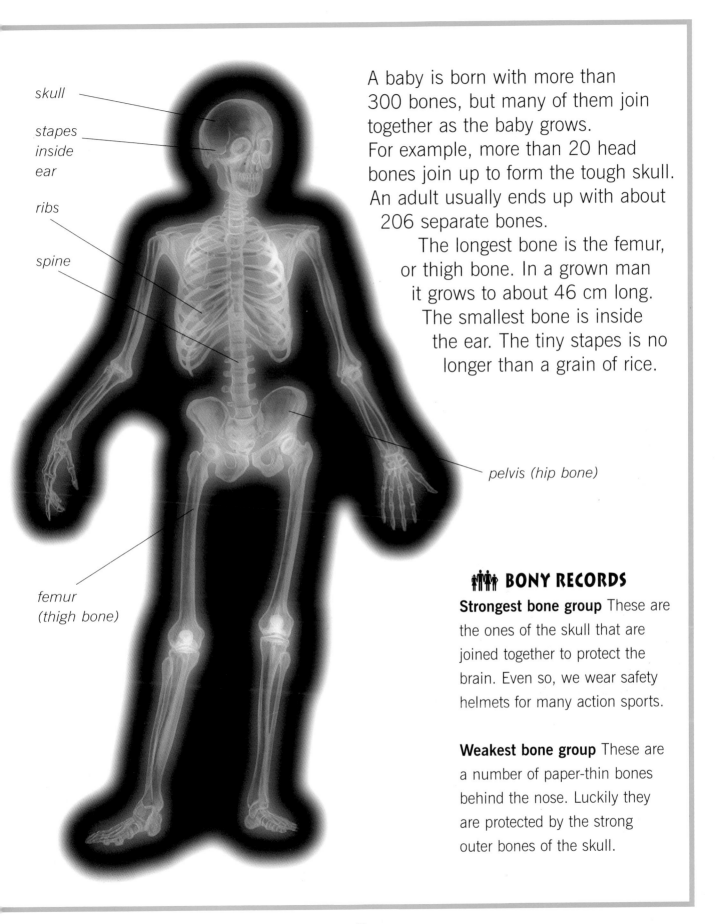

skull

stapes inside ear

ribs

spine

femur (thigh bone)

pelvis (hip bone)

A baby is born with more than 300 bones, but many of them join together as the baby grows. For example, more than 20 head bones join up to form the tough skull. An adult usually ends up with about 206 separate bones.

The longest bone is the femur, or thigh bone. In a grown man it grows to about 46 cm long. The smallest bone is inside the ear. The tiny stapes is no longer than a grain of rice.

👪 BONY RECORDS

Strongest bone group These are the ones of the skull that are joined together to protect the brain. Even so, we wear safety helmets for many action sports.

Weakest bone group These are a number of paper-thin bones behind the nose. Luckily they are protected by the strong outer bones of the skull.

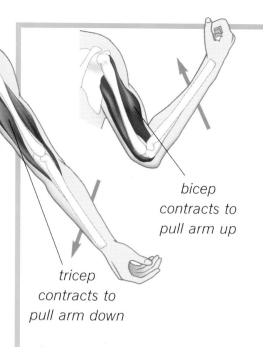

bicep contracts to pull arm up

tricep contracts to pull arm down

▲ Muscles work in pairs to move bones. One muscle pulls your arm up, another pulls it back straight again.

MUSCLE POWER

About 40 per cent of a human's weight is made up of muscles. They move the skeleton and the organs inside the body.

You have more than 600 main muscles, but there are thousands of smaller ones. Every hair has a tiny muscle in the skin that pulls the hair up when it gets cold!

Muscles get bigger when they are exercised regularly. For example, the world's biggest bicep belongs to an American. He lifts buckets of sand for practice and has a bicep nearly 80 cm around – it is even bigger when he flexes it!

◀ You need more than 200 different muscles just to walk. This is because groups of several muscles are used for most movements.

Muscles are made of fibres so small that about 1 million of them would fit inside a 10 mm square. Humans may have lots of main muscles, but many creatures beat our records. For example, a wriggly caterpillar has over 2000!

▲ Regular exercise makes muscle fibres thicker and stronger. Training works for women as well as men – in 2000 a Chinese woman lifted a record weight of 160.5 kg.

👤👤👤 MUSCLE RECORDS

Strongest muscle The masseter is the muscle you use to shut your mouth. It is used for chewing food and for talking.

Smallest muscle The stapedius is part of your hearing system inside the ear and is tiny – it measures just over 1 mm long.

Biggest muscle The gluteus maximus in each buttock straightens your leg when you stand up.

Fastest muscle This is the muscle that blinks your eyelids at up to five times a second to keep the eyes clear of dust.

◄ The face is packed with muscles. A frown uses about 40 muscles, but a smile uses less than half this number.

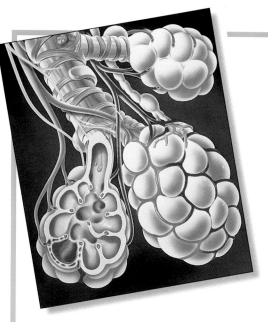

TAKE A BREATH

When you breathe in, you suck air through the nose or mouth. It passes down your windpipe, then it goes into the lungs.

▲ Alveoli are so small that the lungs are packed with 700 million of them. They take oxygen from the air during the 20 000 or so breaths we take daily.

We need air because it contains the gas oxygen, which is essential for life. As you breathe, normally 15–20 times a minute, air goes into your lungs, through a system of fine tubes to grape-like sacs called alveoli. The alveoli take oxygen from the air and pass it into the blood, which is pumped around the body by the heart.

Air moves fastest in the body when you cough or sneeze. Both are caused by particles, such as dust, dirt or pollen, blocking air passages. A big sneeze may have the force of a small tornado. Some researchers claim to have measured brief 'sneeze speeds' through the nose of more than 1000 km/h!

Audrey Ferrera gets ready for a freedive record attempt

👬 HOLD YOUR BREATH!

Deep diver In 2000 Loic Leferme from France set a new freediving record. Using no breathing gear and with heavy weights to sink fast, he went down to 152m before having to return. Also in 2000, Audrey Ferrera set a womens' record of 125m.

Hog hiccups An American pig farmer called Charles Osborne had the worst bout of hiccups ever. In 1922, he hiccuped when weighing a pig – and could not stop for 68 years! Hiccups is a medical mystery – no one knows why we have them.

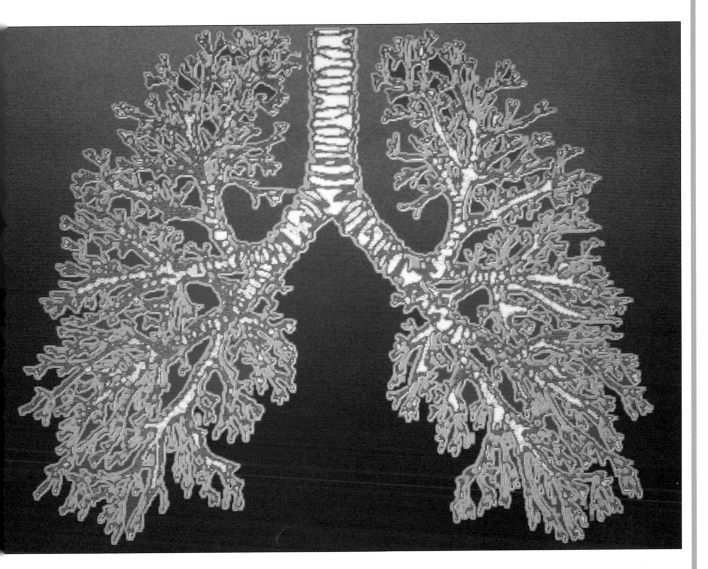

▲ The lungs look rather like trees in this special photograph. If you could lay all the lung surfaces out flat, they would cover an area of more than 80 sq m – that's parking space for 12 medium-sized cars!

◄ We need oxygen but too much of it can cause convulsions. To avoid this, diver Nuno Gomes breathed a special gas mixture called nitrox when he achieved a record depth of almost 283m in 1996.

PUMPING BLOOD

The heart is a muscular pump about the size of a clenched fist. Its job is to keep blood flowing round the body.

▲ Hard exercise boosts blood-flow through the heart up to 20 times.

used blood passes through veins (blue)

fresh blood passes through arteries (red)

valves stop blood being pumped the wrong way

The heart has two halves, each with two chambers. One side pumps blood from the lungs – which have filled it with energy-rich oxygen – to the rest of the body. The other side pumps 'used' blood with little oxygen left in it, back to the lungs.

The heart beats about 80 times a minute in a child, 70 in an adult. An adult has 5–6 litres of blood, which passes round the body in tubes called arteries, veins and tiny capillaries. Laid in a line they would measure more than 100 000 km!

▲ An adult's heart beats more than 100 000 times a day. About 80 ml of blood is pumped with every beat, about 8000 litres a day.

▶ If a heart beats irregularly, an electronic pacemaker can keep it in regular rhythm. A Hungarian man holds the record for the longest time with one pacemaker. By 2002 it had been working for 23 years.

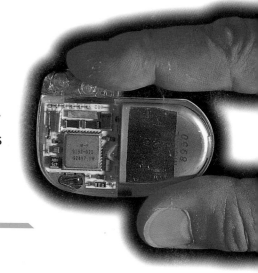

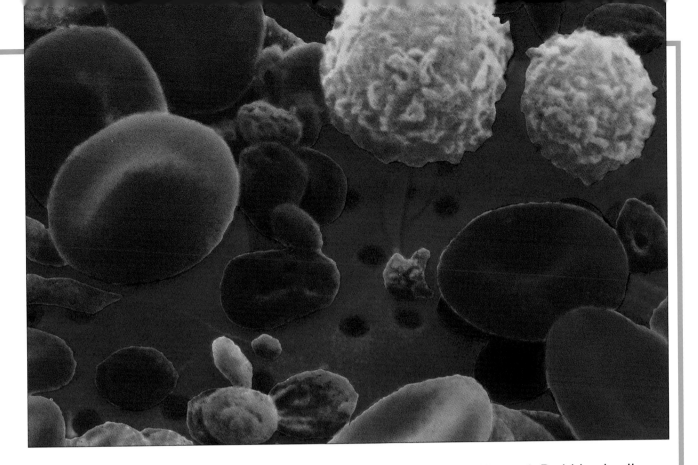

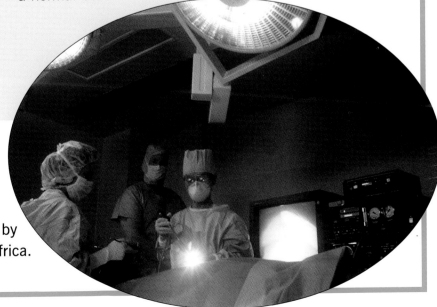

♦♦♦ BLOOD FACTS

Blood bank In 1970, Warren Jyrich was given a record 1080 litres of blood during a long heart operation. This would normally be enough for over 200 people.

White warriors Blood has white blood cells as well as red ones. White cells attack and destroy germs and other intruders.

Heart pump The world's first artificial heart was given to Robert Tools in 2001. He had to get used to a low whirring sound from the electric motor instead of a normal beat.

▲ Red blood cells give blood its colour. There are 5 million of them in every drop.

▶ A surgeon replaces a faulty heart with a healthy one in an operation called a transplant. The first such operation was in 1967, by Dr Christiaan Barnard, in South Africa.

ON THE OUTSIDE

Skin, hair and nails help to protect the body. The skin is a waterproof layer, with nerve cells that respond to touch, hot and cold.

The skin is the biggest human body organ. Spread out in a flat sheet, it would cover an area of nearly 2 sq m. We shed flakes of dead skin all the time. A few grammes a day adds up to an 18-kg heap during a lifetime!

Hairs grow from tiny pits in the skin. Most people have 100 000 hairs on their heads but lose 60–80 of these every day. It is normal to have a regular trim, but a man in Thailand stopped having his hair cut when he was a teenager and he now has the world's longest hair. It is more than 5.18m long!

▲ This microscope view shows a hair growing out of the skin. At top speed a hair can grow nearly 3 mm a week, about three times quicker than fingernails.

👪 BEARD AND NAILS

Bushiest beard When Hans Langseth from Norway died in 1927, his beard was measured at more than 5.33m long. His last trim had been over half a century earlier, in 1876.

Longest nails Shridhar Chillal from India has not cut the nails on his left hand for 50 years. When last measured, his long and curly nails had each grown more than 1m long.

◀ Ugh! It's not an alien invader, but a blood-sucking head louse hanging on to a hair. Imagine 1434 of these little beasts crawling on you – for that's the world record head-louse count!

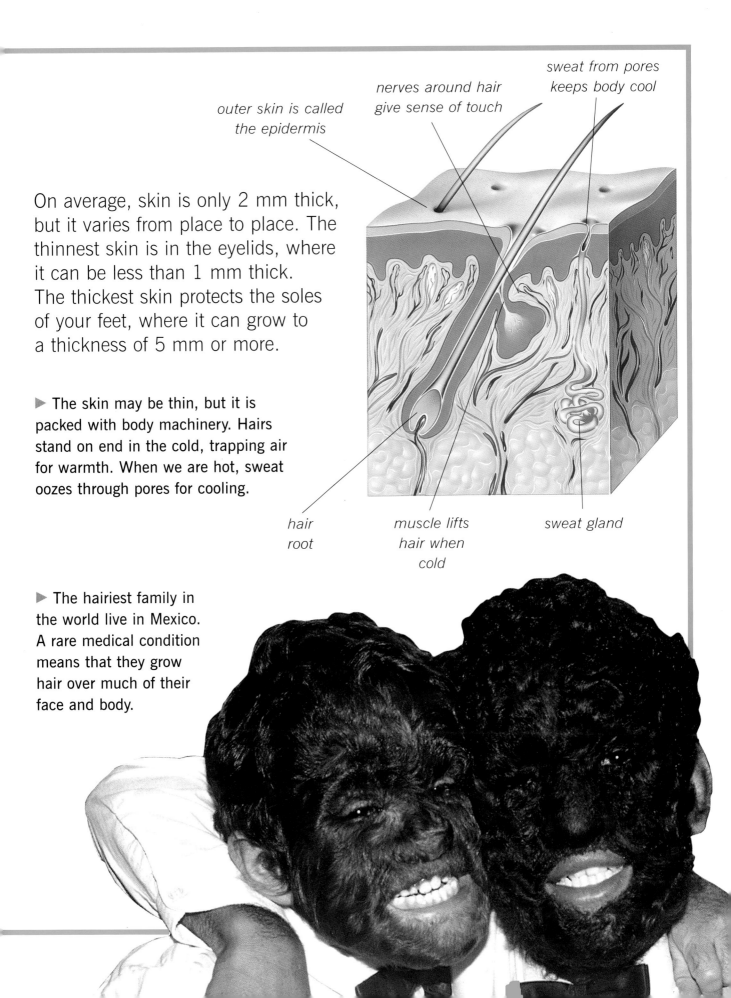

outer skin is called the epidermis

nerves around hair give sense of touch

sweat from pores keeps body cool

On average, skin is only 2 mm thick, but it varies from place to place. The thinnest skin is in the eyelids, where it can be less than 1 mm thick. The thickest skin protects the soles of your feet, where it can grow to a thickness of 5 mm or more.

▶ The skin may be thin, but it is packed with body machinery. Hairs stand on end in the cold, trapping air for warmth. When we are hot, sweat oozes through pores for cooling.

hair root

muscle lifts hair when cold

sweat gland

▶ The hairiest family in the world live in Mexico. A rare medical condition means that they grow hair over much of their face and body.

THOUGHT MACHINE

The brain controls your body. It keeps the heart, lungs, stomach and other organs working properly. And it is the most powerful thinking organ we know.

▲ When it works hard, the brain uses enough energy to make a lightbulb glow. Humans do not have the biggest brains though – those of dolphins, whales and elephants are all heavier.

The brain is the third largest organ in the body, weighing about 1.4 kg in a man, a little less in a woman. It is by far the most complex nervous linkup – there are more than 100 *billion* brain cells, each one of them linked to hundreds or even thousands of others.

The brain weighs only about 2 per cent of the body's total, but it uses 20 per cent of the energy. Oxygen in the blood is vital – if any part of the brain goes without it for more than a few minutes, that part starts to die.

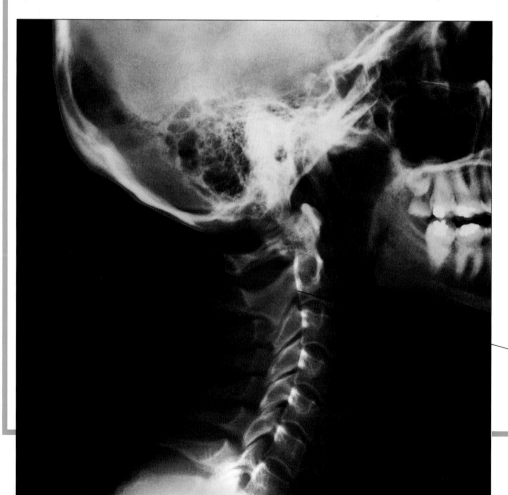

◀ The brain is joined to the body by the spinal cord. This is a bundle of nerves inside the backbone that sends messages as tiny flashes of electricity around the body. The fastest of these hurtle along at more than 400 km/h.

spinal cord is inside the backbone

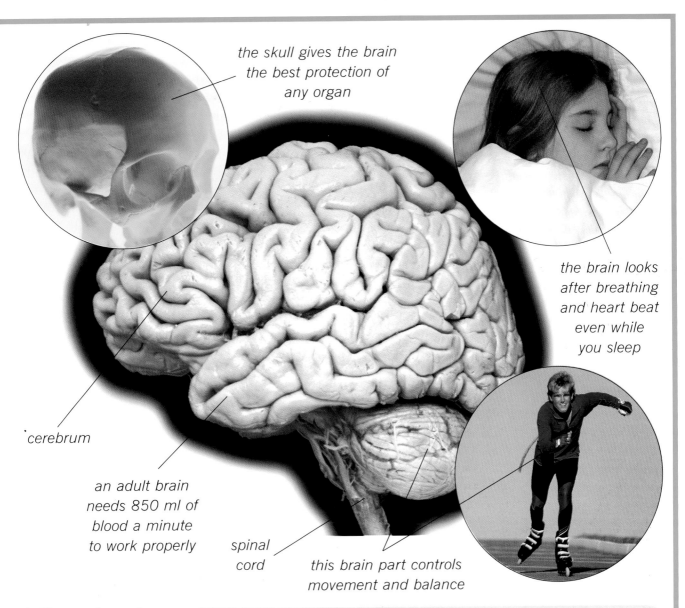

the skull gives the brain
the best protection of
any organ

the brain looks
after breathing
and heart beat
even while
you sleep

cerebrum

an adult brain
needs 850 ml of
blood a minute
to work properly

spinal
cord

this brain part controls
movement and balance

▲ The cerebrum is the biggest part of the brain. This mass of wrinkled tissue is where most thoughts, feelings and emotions occur. Some brain cells are the smallest in the body, with sizes that go down to a tiny 0.005 mm.

👥 BRAIN BUSTERS

Big brain The biggest brain ever measured belonged to a man in the USA. His brain weighed 2.3 kg, nearly twice normal size. The smallest brain belonged to an Irishman – it weighed 680g.

Amazing memory Some people remember things exactly. One of these was Bhandata Vicitsara, who could recall thousands of pages from books, without needing to jog his memory.

Arty fact People who are best at the arts use the left side of their brain most. The right side deals with logical skills such as arithmetic.

EYES AND EARS

You see when light enters your eye through the pupil. Your ears detect sounds and also have organs that help you balance.

▲ Muscles in the eyes are the busiest in the body. The very best eyesight can see about 250 separate colours with 17 000 shades, as well as 300 shades of grey.

retina is covered with rod and cone cells

light passes through the clear pupil

lens focuses light on the retina

optic nerve

Vision takes up the most brain-power of the senses, with about 25 per cent of the brain working to understand what the eyes are seeing. The secret of sight lies with light-sensitive cells in the back of each eye. About 7 million cone-shaped cells work in bright light for colour vision. Around 130 million rod-shaped cells work in dim light but in black and white.

▲ Rod and cones cells on the retina react to light. Signals from the cells pass along the optic nerve to the brain.

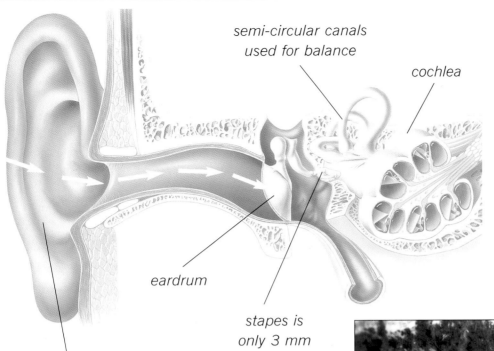

semi-circular canals
used for balance

cochlea

◄ Children have the best hearing – adult ears cannot detect very high-pitched sounds so well. Even the best set of ears can detect little more than about 1500 different tones.

eardrum

stapes is
only 3 mm
long

outer ear
collects
sound

Sound is carried through the air as waves of energy that hit the eardrum and make it vibrate thousands of times a second. The vibrations pass through three tiny bones, including the smallest bone of all, the stapes. The snail-shaped cochlea changes the vibrations to nerve signals, which go to the brain.

Our sense of balance comes from more than 20 000 nerves lining tiny tubes called the semi-circular canals. As we move, liquid sloshes about in the canals – and the nerves detect the slightest movement.

👪 HIGH-WIRE DISPLAY

The greatest balancing feat was by a man called Charles Blondin. In 1859, he walked a tightrope strung 335m above the huge Niagara Falls in North America.

He did this amazing act several times. Once he even stopped in the middle to cook an omelette on a small stove he had carried!

TASTE AND SMELL

We taste with taste buds on the tongue. Smell works by detecting chemicals in the air with the nose. And when we eat we use both senses together.

papillae

▲ The tongue is a strong muscle, with a velvety surface that lets you feel texture in food. Taste buds are found in lumpy bits called papillae.

You have about 10 000 taste buds scattered around your tongue. When you chew, the taste buds react to different chemicals in food and send nerve messages to the brain which decides whether the taste is nice or nasty.

There is no limit on how many tastes there are, but they are all mixed from four kinds of taste – sweet, sour, salty and bitter. Some Japanese scientists add a kind of meaty-savoury taste – they call it *umami*.

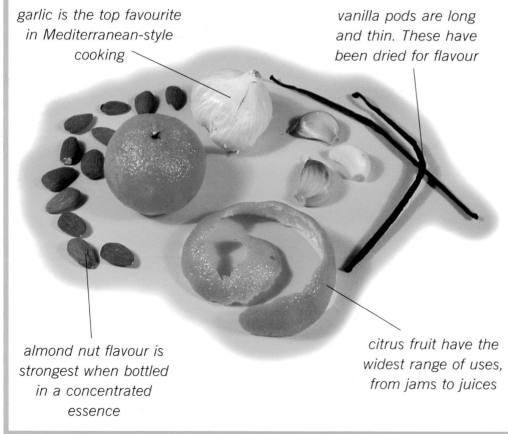

garlic is the top favourite in Mediterranean-style cooking

vanilla pods are long and thin. These have been dried for flavour

almond nut flavour is strongest when bottled in a concentrated essence

citrus fruit have the widest range of uses, from jams to juices

◄ The most popular flavouring is vanilla. It goes into many foods, from cakes to ice cream. People with very good smell and taste often work in the food and drink industry. The world's top noses can tell more than 19 000 odours apart.

🚹🚺 TASTE IT, SMELL IT

Nicest taste Sweet tastes are the most popular, followed closely by salty tastes. This explains why snack makers usually make their foods very sweet or very salty. Salty snacks make you thirsty, and then you might want to have a sweet fizzy drink!

Sensitive smell Even the most sensitive human nose comes off badly when compared to the animal kingdom. Our smell receptors cover an area about the size of a postage stamp and can tell the difference between thousands of smells. But a dog has at least 20 times more smell receptors than a human. And some male moths can detect a female moth 10 km away.

▲ A dog has 200 million smell receptors packed into its nose.

The smelliest substance in the world is a chemical called ethyl mercaptan. It is a mixture of carbon and sulphur so strong that just 2–3 drops would be enough to fill a concert hall with its smell.

We smell using nerves in the nose. Just as taste buds sense chemicals in food, so smell receptors detect particles in the air. Taste and smell are linked closely, so when you have a cold, food loses much of its flavour.

▶ Our smell receptors are in the area shown by this see-through computer scan. They sense chemicals in the air and send nerve messages to the brain.

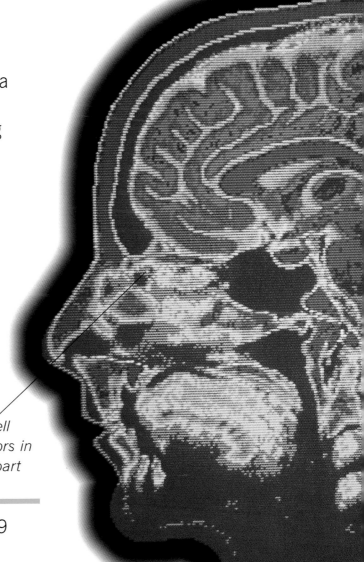

smell receptors in this part

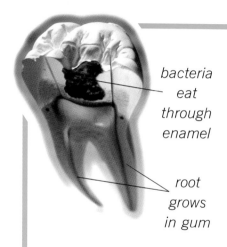

bacteria eat through enamel

root grows in gum

TAKE A BITE

Your body needs energy to work and this comes from food. Humans eat quite a lot – in a lifetime you may chomp through about 40 tonnes of food.

▲ Tooth enamel is the hardest material in the body. But bacteria can still eat through it to create a cavity. If the damage is not repaired, the root can be infected and the tooth will die.

Once you have chewed and swallowed, food goes down your oesophagus to the stomach, a trip that normally takes about 10 seconds.

The stomach is part of the alimentary canal, a 9m-long tube with sections that do different jobs to absorb food. An adult's stomach usually holds about a litre of food and drink, but it can stretch. This probably helped a Japanese man win a hot-dog eating contest – he ate 50 dogs in 12 minutes!

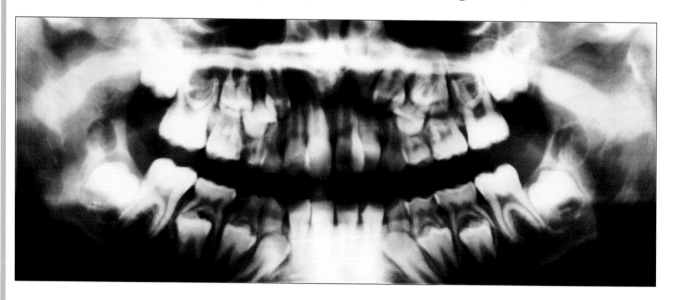

▲ Human teeth grip, tear and chew food. An adult has 32 teeth in a full set.

Food passes through the alimentary canal at a snail's pace. From beginning to end, it is a 24-hour journey before waste passes out of the body. During that time about 9 litres of food and liquid has been digested.

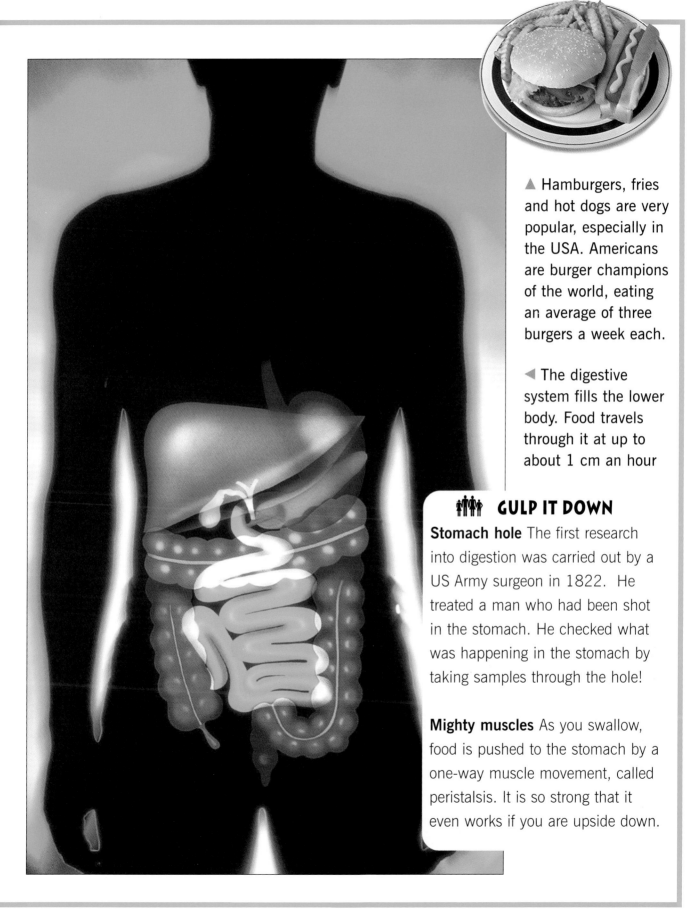

▲ Hamburgers, fries and hot dogs are very popular, especially in the USA. Americans are burger champions of the world, eating an average of three burgers a week each.

◀ The digestive system fills the lower body. Food travels through it at up to about 1 cm an hour

👪 GULP IT DOWN

Stomach hole The first research into digestion was carried out by a US Army surgeon in 1822. He treated a man who had been shot in the stomach. He checked what was happening in the stomach by taking samples through the hole!

Mighty muscles As you swallow, food is pushed to the stomach by a one-way muscle movement, called peristalsis. It is so strong that it even works if you are upside down.

EXTREME PEOPLE

Most humans grow to a fairly similar height and very few of us live to be more than 100 years old. But some people are different.

▲ Jeanne Calment from France holds the age record. She died in 1997, at 122 years 164 days old. The oldest man in recent years was Antonio Todde, an Italian shepherd, who died in 2002 just before his 113th birthday.

The tallest man of the twentieth century was the American Robert Wadlow. By the time he was 21 years old, he was 2.72m tall and weighed 223 kg. Robert was strong, too – as a child he could pick up his father easily! The tallest woman on record came from China – she was 2.48m high.

Women may be shorter than men, but they usually live a few years longer – the world's oldest woman lived for two years more than the oldest man on record. He was a Japanese islander who survived for 120 years.

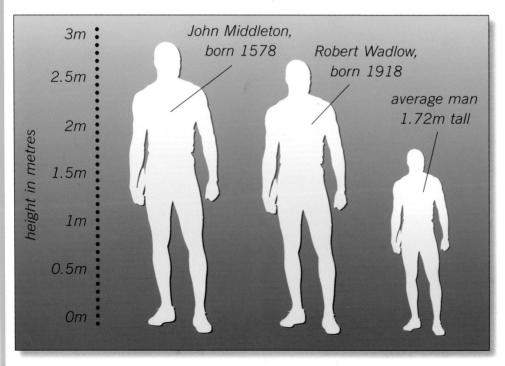

John Middleton, born 1578

Robert Wadlow, born 1918

average man 1.72m tall

height in metres

3m
2.5m
2m
1.5m
1m
0.5m
0m

◄ The tallest man in recent history was the 'gentle giant' Robert Wadlow. But more than 300 years before, another giant lived in Hale, Britain. Records of the time claimed that John Middleton grew to be 2.82m tall.

ᴀ OLDER AND FATTER

Most oldies On average, only about 75 people in a million live to be 100 years old, but nearly twice as many people on the Italian island of Sardinia live for a century. Even more people on Japan's Okinawa island do so. No one knows why this is, but researchers are trying to find out.

Most fatties The islanders of Nauru in the Pacific are the world's fattest people, according to a survey in 2001. Nearly eight in ten of Nauru's adults are overweight. Doctors say it is caused mostly by too many fatty foods and not enough exercise.

▶ The Padaung people of southeast Asia think that long necks are beautiful. Padaung women have the longest necks in the world. They do it by inserting metal hoops one at a time. Over many years, the neck slowly gets longer and longer!

the longest neck on record was 40 cm long

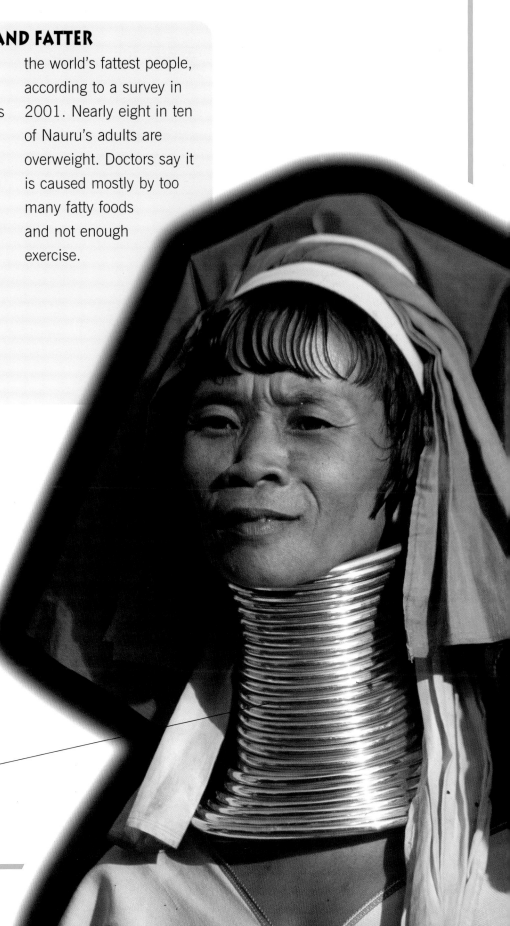

BODY BREAKDOWN

antiseptic spray

▲ Sir Joseph Lister was the first surgeon to tackle disease in hospitals with antiseptic spray, in the 1860s. Until then no one thought that clean hospitals were important.

We are healthy most of the time. Sometimes coughs or colds keep us in bed for a while. But the body can also be attacked by really dangerous diseases.

The deadliest single disease is still the fourteenth-century Black Plague, which killed about one-third of the world's population from 1347 to 1351. In Europe, the Black Plague killed about 40 million people. Today, deaths caused through the HIV virus threaten to overtake the Black Plague. So far, 25 million people have died and experts think the total could pass 60 million by 2010.

Tobacco is the other big killer. Smoking causes all sorts of heart and lung diseases. Worldwide, about 3 million people a year die from tobacco-related diseases.

👪 SNEEZES AND ACHES

Atchoo! You usually sneeze only when you have a cold or hay fever. But the longest sneezing session on record was far worse. In 1981, British girl Donna Griffiths started sneezing and could not stop for over two years.

Oldest medicine Some useful medicine goes back a long time. Over 2400 years ago the Greek Hippocrates found that chewing the bark of a willow tree helped to ease many aches and pains. Today we call the active ingredient aspirin.

▲ Aspirin was first made as a medicine by the German Bayer company in 1899.

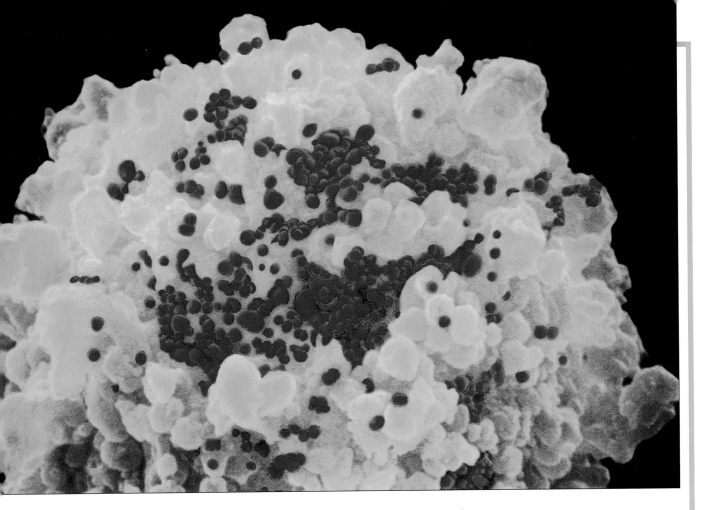

▲ The HIV virus (shown above in red) attacks the body's defences, leaving it open to disease. AIDS is the last stage of infection, when diseases have a firm grip.

▶ The most common disease is the familiar cold, which most of us catch at least once a year and often more. There are nearly 200 types of cold germ, so there are plenty of chances of being infected. You can see from this picture why you should always use a handkerchief!

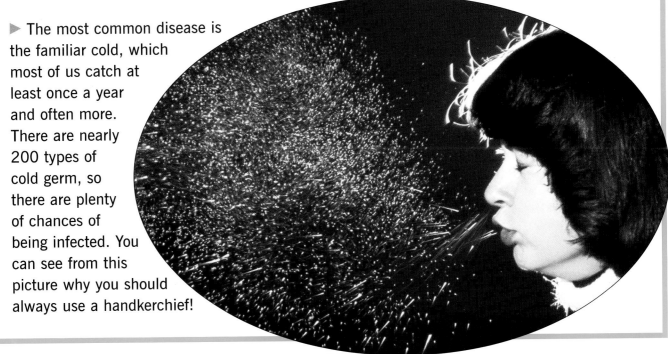

HUMAN BODY RECORDS

egg cell

Here are some facts and records about the human body.

CELL SIZES

Body cells vary widely in size and shape. The female egg is the most bulky, but the longest are nerve cells that stretch from your lower spine to your toes – a distance of about 1.3m.

SWEATY KILLER

Body researchers are always finding something new. One discovery in 2001 was dermcidin, a substance made in the skin. It is mixed in sweat and helps kill bacteria.

SUPER-CHILLY SWIM

An icy underwater record was set in 2000 by Wim Hof from the Netherlands. First, he chopped a hole through the ice of a frozen lake in Finland. Then he jumped in and swam under the ice for a distance of just over 57m, holding his breath for over a minute. And he wore no special clothing!

MOST CELLS

A 2002 study reckoned that the human body is made of about 100 000 000 000 000 cells. However, it's not a fixed amount – the number changes with body size and age.

SPEEDY SURGERY

Before anaesthetics were invented to put you to sleep, operations were painful, so fast surgeons were needed. One of them claimed he could cut off 180 limbs in an hour! Today, things are less painful and about 4 million operations are carried out each year.

◀ Anaesthetic drugs date back to 1842, when ether was first used to send a patient to sleep during an operation. Nitrous oxide (laughing gas) was first used by an American dentist in 1844.

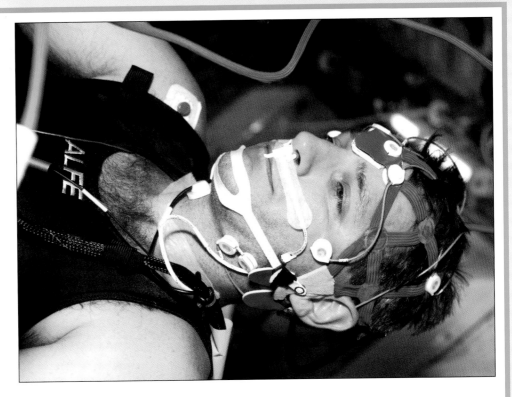

► US astronaut Richard Linnehan wears a 'sleep cap'. It records brain and muscle activity during sleep. In space, the weightless conditions allow an astronaut's spine to stretch about 3–6 cm during a 10-day mission

OLDEST OPERATIONS

The earliest known surgery dates back 7000 years or more. Ancient skulls have been found with holes drilled through the bone. Experts think the holes were drilled to try and relieve agonizing headaches, the idea being to let the pains out. Yikes!

SILENT SLEEPERS

Astronauts are the no-snoring champions. For reasons that no one has yet found out, almost no one snores while asleep on a spacecraft. Back on Earth snoring is often caused when the soft parts at the back of the throat flap against the tongue.

YOUR DAILY SHRINK

People's height varies as the day goes on. You are tallest when you wake up, but during the day the bones in your spine slowly squash together. By the time you go to bed, you are likely to be about 1 cm shorter! At night the spine stretches out again.

Some people are born very small. The shortest man known was Gul Mohammed from India, who was 57 cm high. The shortest woman came from the Netherlands and was born in 1876. Sadly, she died at just 19 years old, when she was just 61 cm tall.

FRIENDS FOR LIFE?

Most humans are home to a very small creature, just 0.3 mm long, called the follicle mite. The mite was discovered in 1842 and it lives in the base of hairs in our eyelashes, noses and other parts. The record found is 25, all on one eyelash root. Follicle mites have eight legs, just right for hanging on!

HUMAN BODY WORDS

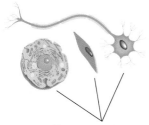

cells come in many shapes and sizes

Here are some words used in this book that you may not know.

ALVEOLI

Tiny air sacs in the lungs that absorb oxygen from the air. They then return waste to the air when we breathe out.

ARTERY

A blood vessel that carries oxygen-rich blood from the heart. Veins return used blood to the heart. Capillaries are the smallest blood vessels.

BACTERIA

Microscopic living things (also known as germs or microbes) that exist almost everywhere. There are thousands of types of bacteria. Some produce disease but many others are useful, such as the ones that change milk to yoghurt.

CELL

The smallest unit of the living body, from which we are made. Cells of many different kinds and shapes carry out all of the body's functions.

ENAMEL

The outer layer of the teeth. It is the body's hardest material.

FREEDIVE

An underwater sport in which a diver aims to go as deep as possible without using any breathing equipment.

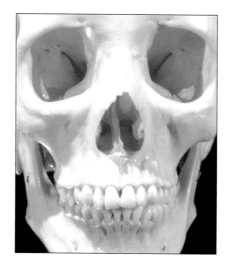

▶ White enamel covers the outside of the teeth.

HIV

A virus that attacks body cells and that often causes AIDS. Once a person has AIDS, their body cannot fight infection.

MARROW

Living material inside a bone that makes red blood cells.

NERVE

A body cell which can carry and transmit an electrical signal. Nerves are the body's messenger system, swapping information and instructions every moment of life.

OPTIC NERVE

The bundle of nerves which carries signals from each eye to the brain.

ORGAN

The name for soft parts of the body such as the stomach, heart, brain, lungs and so on.

OXYGEN

One of the gases that make up the air we breathe. Air is a mixture of mostly nitrogen gas (78 per cent) and oxygen (21 per cent) with traces of various other gases. Oxygen is needed by all living cells in the body and is extracted from the air by alveoli in the lungs.

PACEMAKER

A matchbox-sized electronic machine that sends out an exactly-timed electric signal to keep the heart beating regularly. A pacemaker may be used if the heart's natural pacemaker becomes irregular or fails completely.

PERISTALSIS

The wave-like muscle movement that pushes food along the digestive system.

TRANSPLANT

A surgical operation in which a failed organ, such as a heart or a kidney, is replaced with a good one from another body.

VALVE

Small flaps in the heart that open and shut to keep blood flowing in the correct direction around the body.

VIRUS

A disease-producing organism that lives inside a cell, which

▲ A plastic heart valve may be used to replace a natural one that is faulty or damaged.

it then takes over. The body's defences may fail to spot or attack the virus, which can then spread to other cells.

X-RAY

Radiation that passes through flesh, but is stopped by harder things, like bone. Other types of radiation include light, radio and microwaves.

▶ An x-ray photo through the chest shows the ribs and an electronic pacemaker, in place to keep the heart beating regularly.

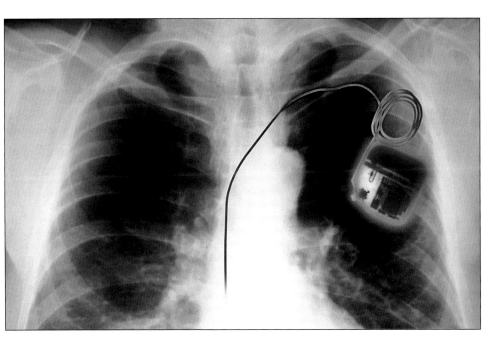

HUMAN BODY PROJECTS

These two experiments show you some human body science.

A very important thing for our bodies is to be neither too hot nor too cold. In chilly weather we can wear thicker clothes for insulation, or protection, from the cold. In hot weather we can stay cool by taking clothes off. Then sweat can help keep us cool by taking away heat by evaporation.

◀ We may need several layers of clothing to insulate us in cold weather, such as winter snow.

INSULATION FOR WARMTH

Insulation works by trapping layers of warm air against the skin. Furry animals have natural insulation, but humans have to wear clothes to do the same job. In this experiment you can find out how layers of insulation can help in chilly places.

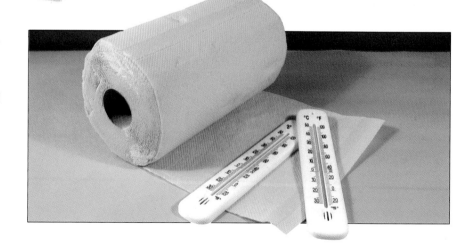

1 You need a roll of kitchen paper and two greenhouse thermometers. You will also need to be able to use some free space in a freezer for about 30 minutes.

COOLING BY EVAPORATION

Evaporation is when water turns to tiny droplets of water vapour, such as when puddles dry in sunshine. When body moisture evaporates into the air, heat is taken with it, so you feel cooler.

◄ Lightweight clothing allows the breeze to cool this runner.

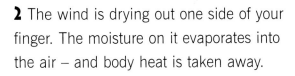

1 All you need is a finger and some wind. Lick your finger and hold up against the breeze. You will feel the windy side is cooler.

2 The wind is drying out one side of your finger. The moisture on it evaporates into the air – and body heat is taken away.

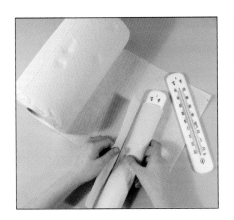

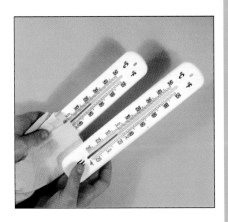

2 Check the thermometers are the same temperature, then wrap one in layers of paper.

3 Fix the paper with tape if needed, then place the two thermometers in the freezer.

4 After 30 minutes check the thermometers. The insulated one should be much warmer.

INDEX